Contents

Superhero Mask

Discover your hidden superpowers when you wear this stunning superhero mask.

You will need:

* pencil and thin white paper (for tracing the templates)
* A4 sheet of blue craft foam
* sewing pins * scissors * pen
* A4 sheet of red craft foam
* A4 sheet of yellow craft foam
* craft glue and paintbrush
* hole punch
* 25cm length of thin elastic

1 Trace the mask template on page 27 onto thin white paper and cut it out. Pin it to the blue foam and draw around the shape using the pen.

2 Cut out the mask shape and the eye holes. Remove the pins and the template.

3 Trace the star template on page 27 onto thin white paper and cut it out. Pin it to the red foam and draw around the shape.

4 Cut out the star shape and the circle in the middle. Remove the pins and the template. Repeat to make a second star.

5 Trace the lightning flash template on page 27 onto thin white paper and cut it out. Pin it to the yellow foam and draw around the shape.

6 Cut out the lightning flash shape. Remove the pin and the template. Repeat to make a second lightning flash.

7 Glue a red star over one of the eye holes so that the holes match up. Repeat to add the other foam star.

8 Glue the lightning flashes onto either side of the mask, as shown above.

9 Use the hole punch to make a hole on either side of the mask. Pass one end of the piece of elastic through one of the holes and knot it to the rest of the elastic.

10 Pass the other end of the elastic through the other hole. Ask an adult to adjust the elastic to fit your head and knot it through the second hole. Trim off any extra elastic.

You will have enough craft foam left to make a mask for another superhero!

Chinese Mask

This style of mask is worn by some Chinese opera singers. The colours of the mask show that the character in the opera is a very brave person.

You will need:

* balloon
* newspaper torn into small pieces
* bowl
* white glue mixed with the same amount of water
* pencil
* paintbrush * scissors
* pencil and thin white paper (for tracing the template)
* thin card
* white paint, red paint, black paint and gold paint
* thin elastic
* hole punch

1 Blow up the balloon and tie the end. Balance the balloon in a bowl with the tied end at the bottom. Paint some of the glue mixture onto the front half of the balloon and stick on pieces of newspaper, overlapping the pieces as shown. Continue until half the balloon is covered with two or three layers of overlapping newspaper. Leave to dry overnight.

2 Pop the balloon. Trim the rough edges of the papier-mâché mask shape. Hold it up to your face and ask someone to use a pencil to mark the position of your eyes. Cut out eye holes and a mouth shape, as shown above. You might need to ask an adult for help with this.

3 Using thin paper and a pencil, trace the template on page 26 and cut it out. Use it to trace and cut out a nose shape from the thin card. Fold it in half along the dotted line and fold back the flaps.

4 Brush glue onto the flaps and press them onto the centre of the mask with the point between the eyes, as shown.

5 Glue more newspaper strips over the nose shape. Leave to dry overnight.

6 Paint the mask white and leave it until dry. Paint the red part of the design as shown in the photos and leave it until dry.

7 Paint the black part of the design as shown. Leave it to dry. Paint the gold details and leave it to dry.

8 Use the hole punch to make a hole half way down either side of the mask. Thread the elastic through one hole and knot the end to the rest of the elastic. Thread the other end of the elastic through the other hole. Ask an adult to help you adjust the elastic to fit your head. Knot the elastic as before.

Fairy Mask

Turn yourself into a fantastic fairy with this glittering mask.

You will need:

* pencil and A4 sheet of thin white paper (for tracing the template)
* A4 acetate sheet (available from craft shops)
* masking tape
* net fabric, 150mm x 250mm
* glitter glue pens – silver, gold and pink
* scissors
* thin green ribbon

To make this mask you will need to use the table or work surface for two days. Before you begin, check that it is not needed for anything else.

1 Trace the template on page 26 onto the A4 paper. Cut out the fairy wing shape and the eye holes.

2 Place the fairy wing shape on the table top or work surface. Tape the acetate sheet onto the work surface, covering the fairy wing shape. Tape the net on top of the acetate.

3 Trace around the outline of the shape with the gold glitter glue pen.

4 Trace around the eye holes with silver glitter glue. Draw swirly patterns with the gold, silver and pink glitter glue pens. Leave to dry for two days.

5 Carefully peel the decorated net away from the acetate. Use scissors to cut around the outside of your decorated fairy wings.

6 Trim away the net on the inside of the eye holes. You may need to ask an adult to help you do this.

7 Ask an adult to snip a small hole on each side of the mask with scissors. Thread a piece of thin ribbon through one hole and tie it in a knot. Repeat on the opposite side. Put the mask on. Tie the ribbons behind your head.

Pirate Mask

Ahoy me hearties! Have some pirate fun in this perfect pirate mask.

You will need:

* pencil and thin white paper (for tracing the templates)
* scissors
* A4 sheet of stiff red paper
* A4 sheet of stiff flesh-coloured paper
* glue and spreader
* A4 sheet of stiff white paper
* A4 sheet of stiff black paper
* hole punch
* thin black elastic

This mask would be great for a pirate party. Use different coloured papers for the bandana to make masks for all your guests!

1 Trace the pirate templates on page 28 using the thin white paper and cut them out. Draw around the templates on the red paper and cut out the red bandana and the two pieces of the knot.

2 Now trace the mask template on page 28 and use it to cut out a mask from the flesh-coloured paper.

3 Spread glue along the bottom edge of the bandana and stick it to the top of the mask.

4 Using the circle template for the knot, draw around it six times on stiff white paper. Cut out the paper circles and glue them onto the bandana, as shown above.

5 To make the knot, glue the red paper circle you cut out in step 1 onto the other red piece of paper as shown.

6 Glue the paper knot onto the bandana.

7 Trace and use the template on page 28 to cut out an eye-patch from the black paper. Cut a 1-cm-wide strip of black paper from the long side of the sheet of paper. Glue the paper strip and eye-patch onto the mask.

8 Trim the black strip to fit.

9 Use the hole punch to punch a hole on either side of the mask. Thread elastic through the hole and tie it to the rest of the elastic. Ask an adult to help you adjust the elastic to fit and knot it through the other hole.

Dragon Mask

Act out your favourite tales of knights and dragons with this fire-breathing dragon mask.

You will need:

* pencil and A4 sheet of thin white paper (for tracing the template)
* A4 sheet of thin white card
* cardboard egg box for six eggs
* scissors
* dark green, light green and yellow tissue paper torn into small pieces
* glue mixed with the same amount of water
* paintbrush
* red paint
* strong glue
* sheets of orange, red and yellow tissue paper
* yellow paper
* hole punch
* ribbon

1 Trace the template on page 31 using thin white paper and cut it out. Draw around it and cut out the monster head shape from thin card. Ask an adult to help you cut out the eye holes and the mouth.

A   B

2 Cut the top (A) off the egg box. Cut the bottom of the egg box (B) across one of the slots for eggs as shown in the picture. Trim the top of the egg box to match the bottom in size.

3 Paint some of the glue mixture onto the outside of the egg box. Start sticking on strips of green and yellow tissue paper, overlapping the pieces as shown. Continue until the box is covered in a layer of coloured tissue paper. Repeat with the top of the egg box. Leave to dry.

4 Paint the inside of the boxes with red paint. Leave to dry.

5 Trace the teeth template on page 31 using thin white paper and cut it out. Draw around it and use it to cut out card teeth. With the points facing upwards, glue the teeth inside the top of the egg box (A).

6 Using strong glue stick the cut edge of the two halves of the egg box onto the bottom of the mask as shown above.

7 Use the discarded egg box pieces to create dragon eyes. Cut a hole in each one, as shown. Glue the cut edges onto the mask on either side of the nose, over the eye holes.

8 Cover the mask and egg-box eyes with a layer of glue and overlapping tissue paper pieces, as you did in step 3. Leave to dry. Use the template on page 31 to cut out two rings of yellow paper. Glue them onto the eyes, matching up the holes.

9 Trace and cut out the flame template on page 31. Use it to cut out two orange, two yellow and two red flame shapes from the tissue paper.

10 Twist an orange, a yellow and a red tissue flame together, as shown. Repeat. Glue the twisted ends of the flames onto the front of the egg box mouth.

11 Use a hole punch to make a hole on either side of the mask. Thread the end of the ribbon through one of the holes and knot it. Repeat on the opposite side. Put the mask on. Tie the ribbons behind your head.

13

Bird Mask

See the world through the eyes of this exotic bird. Where do you think it lives?

You will need:

* pencil and A4 sheet of thin white paper (for tracing the template)
* A4 sheet of thin yellow card
* hole punch
* scissors
* glue
* A4 sheet of stiff orange paper
* A4 sheet of stiff blue paper
* A4 sheet of stiff purple paper
* 2 x 25cm lengths of narrow green polka dot ribbon

1 Trace the mask template on page 29 onto thin white paper and cut it out. Draw around the template on yellow card and cut out the mask and the eye holes. Use the hole punch to make a hole on either side of the mask.

2 Trace and cut out the feather templates on page 29. Use the biggest one to trace and cut out three large paper feathers from the orange paper. Glue the straight edge of the feathers to the mask, as shown.

3 Use the medium-sized feather template to trace and cut out 18 medium-sized paper feathers from the blue paper. Glue the straight edge of nine feathers around one of the eye holes, as shown. Repeat on the other side.

4 Use the small feather template to trace and cut out 14 small paper feathers from the purple paper. Glue the straight edge of seven feathers around each eye hole, as shown above.

5 Trace and cut out the ring template on page 29 and use it to cut two rings from the thick orange paper. Glue a paper ring over each eye hole, lining up the holes.

6 Use the beak template on page 29 to cut out a beak shape from yellow card. Fold the shape in half down the middle.

7 Open out the card beak. Fold down the flaps on either side of the beak.

8 Glue the flaps on the card beak to the bird mask, placing the beak between the eyes, as shown.

9 Thread a length of ribbon through one of the holes. Tie it in a knot. Repeat on the other side.

Monster Mask

Have some monster fun in this green monster mask and make your friends green with envy.

1 Trace the mask template on page 28 onto thin white paper. Cut it out and pin it onto the square of green craft foam, as shown. Draw around it and don't forget the eye holes. Cut away the bottom part of the foam and the eye holes. Remove the pins and the template.

You will need:

* pencil and thin white paper (for tracing the templates)
* green craft foam, 180mm x 180mm
* black craft foam, 180mm x 70mm
* scissors
* sewing pins
* glue
* glue brush
* 2 pieces of silver card, 50mm x 40mm
* clear tape
* black craft foam, 40mm x 40mm
* ballpoint pen
* hole punch
* thin elastic

2 Cut triangles along the long edge of the black foam to create hair.

3 Brush glue onto the black foam strip, as shown.

4 Glue the black foam strip onto the top (straight edge) of the green foam mask.

5 Use the template on page 26 to cut two bolt shapes from the silver card. Tape them to the back of the mask, half way down, so the silver side faces forward, as shown.

6 Cut out a ring of black foam to fit around one of the monster's eyes. Glue the ring onto the right eye, lining up the edges.

7 Use the pen to draw stitches across the head and over one eye.

8 Use the hole punch to make a hole on either side of the mask. Thread one end of the elastic through a hole and knot it to the elastic. Ask an adult to help you adjust the elastic to fit. Secure it with a knot through the other hole.

Cat Mask

No one will recognise you in this cute cat mask. Purrrfect for a fancy dress party!

1 Trace the template on page 30 and cut it out. Pin it onto the black fur fabric.

2 Cut around the shape. You may need to ask an adult to help you cut out the eyes. Remove the pins and template.

3 Use the cat mask template again. This time pin it onto the black felt.

4 Cut out the shape. Remove the pins and template.

5 Spread glue onto the felt cat shape.

6 Press the paper template onto the felt, matching up the edges. Take the lengths of ribbon. Tape the end of each piece of ribbon onto each side of the mask.

7 Spread glue onto the back of the fur cat shape. Press the glued side onto the paper cat shape, trapping the end of each ribbon inside. Leave to dry.

8 Twist the sparkly, green pipe cleaners together in the middle to form an X. Place them on the furry side of the cat mask, as shown.

9 Use the template on page 30 to cut out a nose from the pink felt. Spread glue onto one side. Press it onto the cat mask over the centre of the pipe cleaners as shown.

10 Use the template on page 30 to cut out two ears from the pink felt. Spread glue onto one side of each shape. Press them onto the fur fabric as shown in the picture on the right. Leave to dry.

Crazy Glasses

Surprise your friends and raise some eyebrows with this pair of wacky glasses.

You will need:

* pencil and thin white paper (for tracing the templates)
* blue sparkly card
* scissors
* clear tape
* stick-on stars
* pink sparkly card
* 2 googly eyes
* thin white card
* measuring tape

If you do not have any sparkly card use plain coloured card. Paint on a thin layer of glue and sprinkle on some glitter.

1 Fold the thin white paper in half, unfold it and place it over the template for the glasses on page 30. Trace the template and cut it out. Unfold the template and draw around it onto the sparkly blue card.

2 Cut out the card glasses, including the eye holes.

3 Trace the eyebrow template on page 30 onto white paper and cut it out. Draw around the template onto the sparkly purple card. Turn the template over and repeat to create a second eyebrow. Cut them both out. They should look like the ones above.

4 Tape the end of each eyebrow onto the back of the glasses, as shown.

5 Decorate the blue glasses with stick-on stars.

6 Trace the eye template on page 30 and cut it out. Use it to draw and cut out a spiral of pink sparkly card. Repeat to make a second spiral.

7 Stick a googly eye into the centre of each pink card spiral.

8 Tape the end of each card spiral to the back of the glasses, as shown.

9 Measure around your head, just above your eyes. Cut a 2-cm strip of thin card 2cm longer than the measurement. Bend the strip into a circle. Overlap the ends by 2cm and tape them together.

10 Tape the ring of paper onto the back of the glasses.

Carnival Mask

Bright colours, sparkle, glitter, feathers and jewels – everything you need to make a fantastic carnival mask.

You will need:

* pencil and thin white paper (for tracing the template)
* A4 sheet of red sparkly card
* gold glitter glue pen
* green glitter glue pen
* small packet of tiny beads
* one large feather
* six smaller feathers
* clear sticky tape
* sparkly pencil – if you don't have a sparkly pencil, use an ordinary pencil and paint it or wrap ribbon around it

The streets of Venice in Italy are filled with people wearing masks during their carnival celebrations each year.

1 Trace the template on page 29 onto thin white paper. Cut it out. Cut around the inside of the eye holes.

2 Draw around the template onto the red sparkly card.

3 Cut out the mask. Repeat to cut out a second card mask.

4 Use the gold glitter glue pen to draw lines across one of the card masks as shown. Use this photo and the large picture at the bottom of the page as a guide.

5 Draw a line of green glitter glue around the outside edge of the mask. Outline the eye holes with glitter glue.

6 While the glitter glue is still wet, sprinkle it with tiny beads. Leave the mask to dry overnight. Shake off any beads that have not stuck to the mask.

7 Tape the feathers onto the back of the mask in the centre.

8 Spread glue onto the back of the second mask shape. Press the glued side onto the back of the decorated mask, trapping the ends of the feathers inside. Leave to dry.

9 Tape the pencil to the side of the mask.

Paper Plate Masks

Create a whole collection of animal disguises using some paper plates and a bit of imagination.

Basic mask

1 Trace the mask template on page 28 onto thin white paper. Cut it out. Place the template onto the back of a paper plate. Draw inside the eye holes of the template and cut them out.

To make a basic paper plate mask you will need:

* pencil and thin white paper (for tracing the template)

* paper plate * scissors

(For the elastic fitting)

* hole punch and a length of thin elastic

(For the hand-held mask)

* pencil * sticky tape

AND

For the lion:

* yellow paint and paintbrush

* glue * 4 strips of orange paper, 210mm x 70mm

* felt-tip pens

For the bear:

* brown paint and paintbrush

* strong glue * two paper cups

* pink paper

* thin white card

2 Instructions for a mask held on by elastic.
Use the hole punch to punch a hole on either side of the mask. Thread the elastic through one hole and tie it in a knot. Thread the other end of the elastic through the other hole. Adjust the elastic to fit your head. Knot the elastic onto the mask.

3 Instructions for a hand-held mask.
Tape the pencil to the back of the mask. Tape it in the centre or to the side.

Lion

A Paint the plate yellow. Leave it to dry. Follow step 1 on page 24 and cut out the eye holes.

B Make 50mm long cuts in the strips of orange paper 10mm apart. Curl the edges using a pencil. Glue the uncut edge of the paper strips onto the back of the plate, around the edge.

C Draw on the lion's nose and mouth with felt-tip pens, as shown. Draw around the eyes. Finish off with elastic (step 2) or tape on a pencil (step 3).

Bear

a Paint the plate brown. Leave it to dry. Follow step 1 on page 24 and cut out eye holes.

b Glue the open end of the paper cup onto the centre of the plate under the eyes. Paint it brown.

c Draw around the open end of a paper cup on thin white card. Repeat. Cut out the paper circles and paint them brown. Leave to dry. Draw around the narrow end of the cup on the pink paper. Repeat. Cut out two pink paper circles.

d Glue the pink circles onto the brown circles. Use the nose template on page 28 to cut out a paper nose in pink paper.

e Glue the paper nose onto the end of the paper cup. Glue the paper ears onto either side of the top of the plate, as shown.

f Draw on a mouth. Finish off with elastic (step 2) or tape on a pencil (step 3).

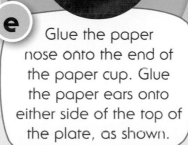

25

Templates

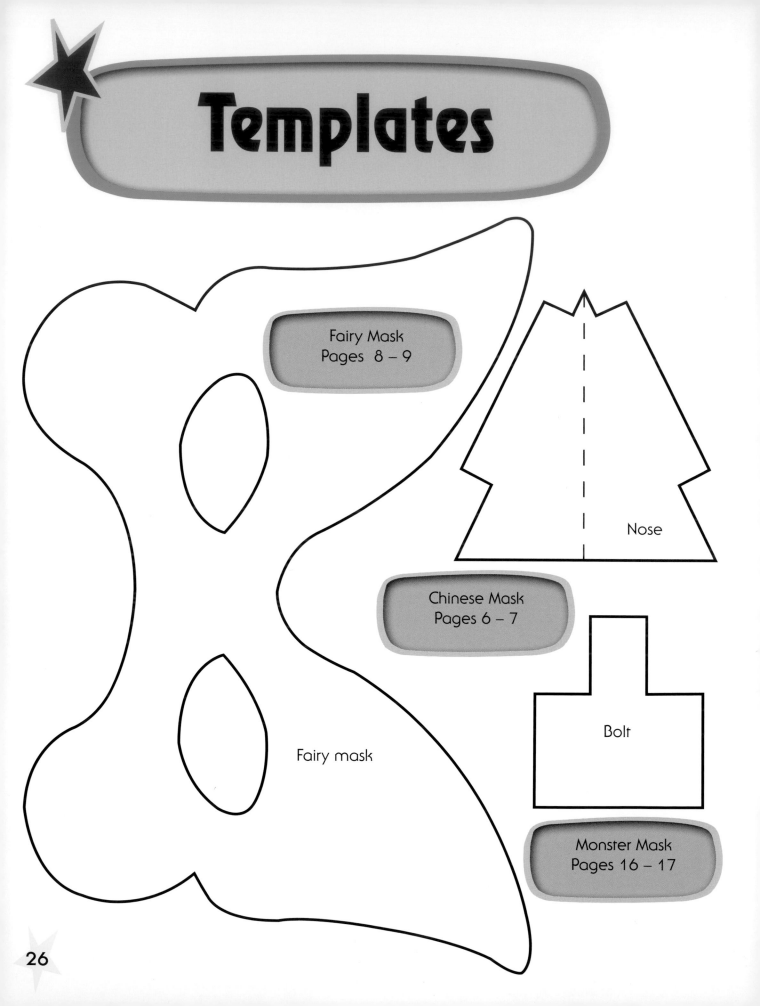

Fairy Mask
Pages 8 – 9

Nose

Chinese Mask
Pages 6 – 7

Bolt

Fairy mask

Monster Mask
Pages 16 – 17

Star

Superhero Mask
Pages 4 – 5

Mask

Lightning flash

You'll need to cut two foam stars and two foam lightning flashes using these templates.

27

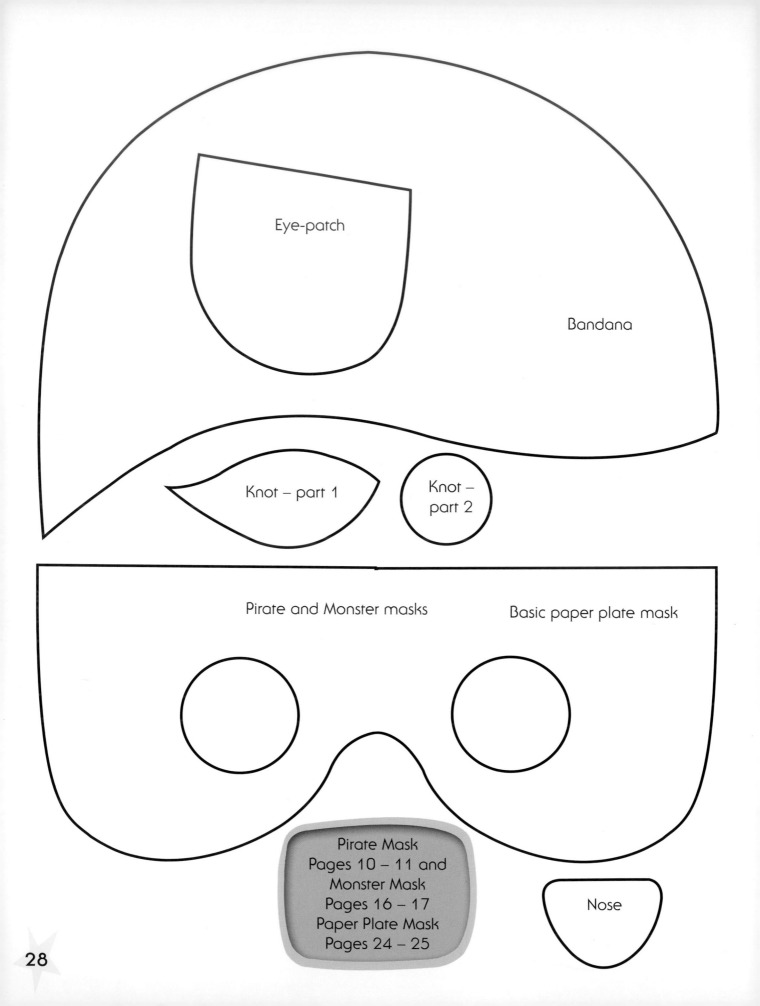

Eye-patch

Bandana

Knot – part 1

Knot – part 2

Pirate and Monster masks

Basic paper plate mask

Pirate Mask
Pages 10 – 11 and
Monster Mask
Pages 16 – 17
Paper Plate Mask
Pages 24 – 25

Nose

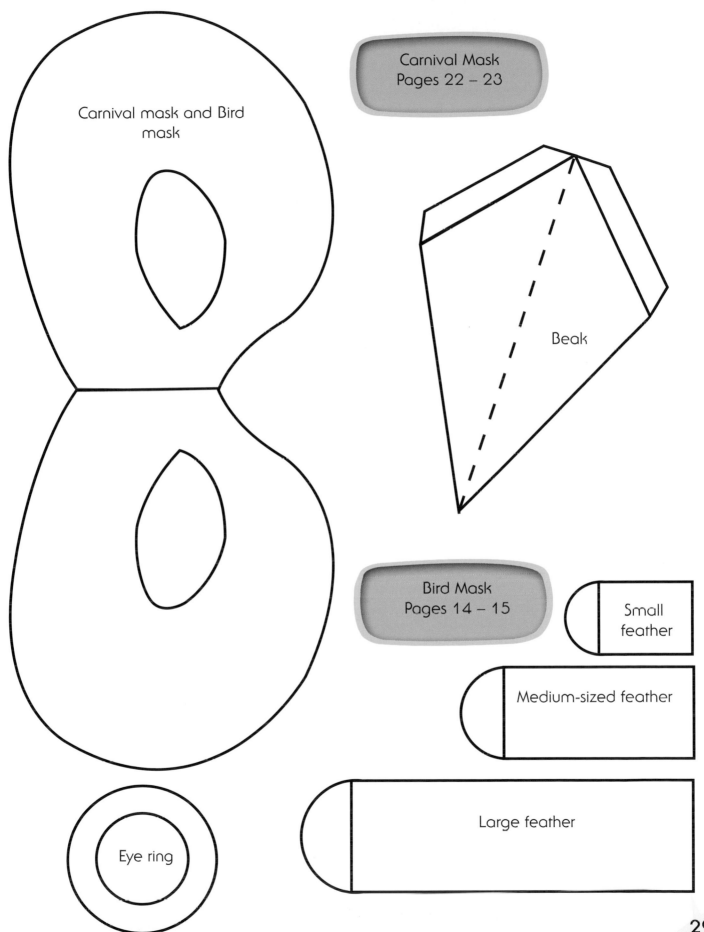

Carnival mask and Bird mask

Carnival Mask
Pages 22 – 23

Beak

Bird Mask
Pages 14 – 15

Small feather

Medium-sized feather

Large feather

Eye ring

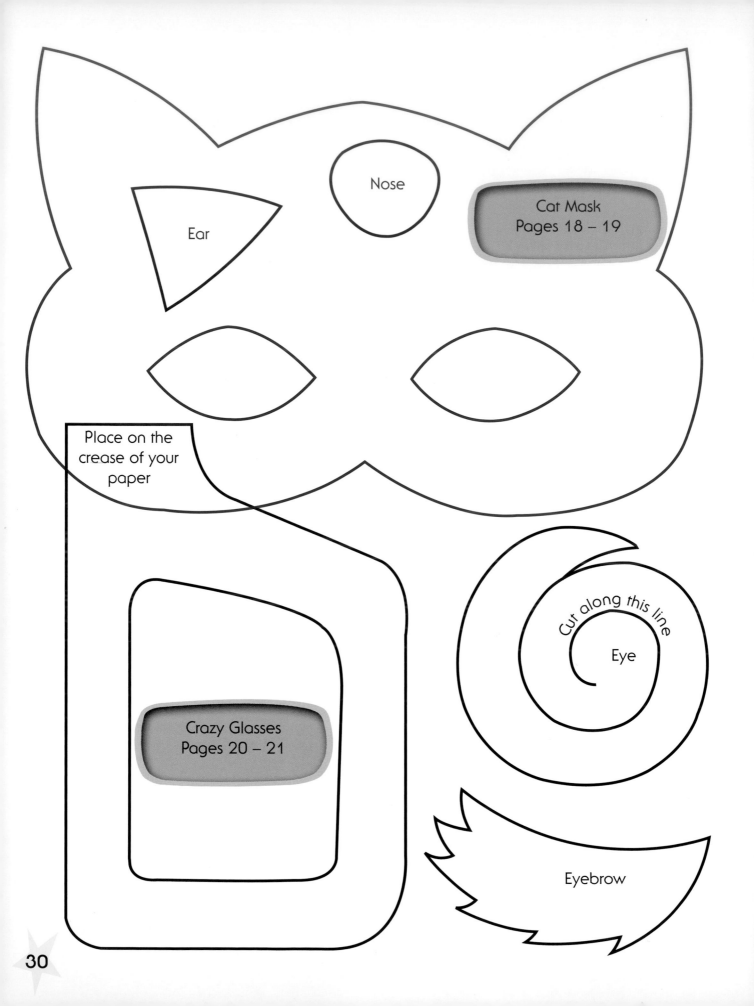

Nose

Ear

Cat Mask
Pages 18 – 19

Place on the crease of your paper

Crazy Glasses
Pages 20 – 21

Cut along this line

Eye

Eyebrow

30

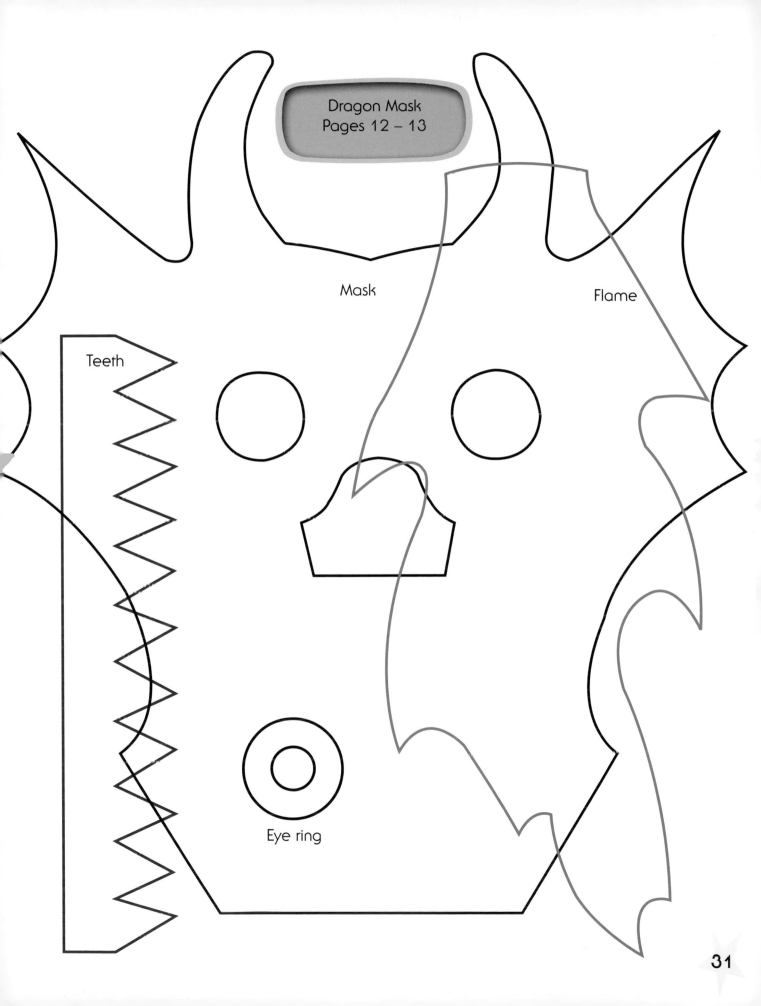

Dragon Mask
Pages 12 – 13

Mask

Flame

Teeth

Eye ring

Index

Further Information

Websites

www.bakerross.co.uk/arts-and-crafts/arts-crafts-masks
This company sell all the craft supplies you might need
to make your masks.

Books

World of Design: Masks by Ruth Thomson (Franklin Watts, 2011) This book
links crafted objects from all around the world to step-by-step projects for
readers to create their own.
Make your own art: Making Masks by Sally Henry and Trevor Cook
(Franklin Watts, 2011) This book is packed with imaginative
easy-to-follow projects.